THE WORLD OF MY POEMS

ANAYA N DANANI

Made with ♥ on the Notion Press Platform
www.notionpress.com

Dedicated to - My mother. This is my gift to you on your Birthday Mom!

Contents

Contents

Foreword

Poetry is the voice of the soul, and when it comes from the heart of a ten-year-old girl, it becomes a pure and unfiltered reflection of how she sees the world. This collection of poems isn't just a book; it's a journey through the eyes of a child—filled with wonder, curiosity, and innocence.

Each poem in this book captures a moment, a thought, or a feeling that reveals the beauty in everyday life.Her words invite us to slow down and notice the small miracles we often overlook. Her unique perspective reminds us that the world is still full of magic if we take the time to see it.

This isn't poetry crafted with rules or formulas; it's poetry that flows naturally from her experiences and imagination. These are the thoughts of a child who is discovering the world, asking questions, and expressing emotions with a raw honesty that is rare and precious.

As you explore these pages, you'll find yourself reconnecting with the simple joys and heartfelt emotions that only childhood can bring. This collection is a celebration of innocence, creativity, and the beauty of seeing the world with fresh eyes. Let these poems remind you to find wonder in the ordinary and joy in the small things around you.

1. Introduction

For the past three years, Anaya has been pouring her thoughts and feelings into her furry pink unicorn diary. Whether she was playing, studying, or watching her favorite shows, inspiration would strike her like a flash of magic. She would rush to her play castle, grab her diary, and eagerly scribble down her thoughts. This diary was her secret treasure, shared only with the most trusted person in her life—her father. Together, they worked on what seemed like a secret mission.Now, after months of effort and collaboration, the pages of Anaya's fluffy pink diary have transformed into what she calls her mother's birthday gift: The World of My Poems.

Through these unfiltered verses, Anaya paints vivid emotions and moments from her life. Her poems celebrate the joy of sibling laughter, the thrill of stepping out into the world, and the quiet, reflective peace of solitude. From the excitement of Christmas holidays in the Alps to the simple joy of lemonade on a sunny day, her poetry is a heartfelt celebration of childhood. This collection is a delightful tapestry of wonder, innocence, and adventure, inviting readers into a world of boundless possibilities.

2. Let it go

Let it go, let it go,
Let it go, let it go,
Just look at it and say "I know"
Let it go. (long)

Let the bygones be the bygones
Let surprises be surprises
Let the future be the future
Let the past be the past
And then let it go, let it go.

Let it go, let it flow,
Let it go with the flow
Just look at it and say "I know"
Let it go. (long)

3. Bhaiya

The one who helps me through,
it's you bhaiya you!
My best buddy though everything
Giving me lots of luck
It's you, Bhaiya you!
Sometimes quite mischievous,
Sometimes a lot too!
But very kind and helpful
It's you, Bhaiya you!

4. The Odd One Out

I like to be special,
I like to be different,
I like to be the odd one out.
(2 times)
When I'm the odd one out,
I feel happy, happy, happy.
When I'm special, I feel special.
When I'm different, I feel different
When I'm the odd one out
I feel like the odd one out
I like to be special
I like to be different
I like to be the odd one out
(2 times)

5. All Along

All alone in the woods,
How would you feel?
If you had somebody with you

All along (hey!)
All along (hey!)
If you had somebody
All along (hey!)
All along (hey!)

How would you feel at that time?
Many people have cursed you,
Many people dislike you,
Many people have taught you a lesson.
But you still haven't bothered to change.
All along (hey!)
All along (hey!)
If you had somebody
All along (hey!)
All along (hey!)
How would you feel at that time?

6. What else can I do?

I feel like I can do nothing else,
than lazing around.
I have no job,
I can't do anything.
What else can I do?
Everyone may have different answers
Oh, what else can I do?
I can't talk to her, can't talk to you.
What else can I do?
Oh, please tell me
Can't talk to her,
Can't talk to you.
WHAT ELSE CAN I DO?(long)

7. Up or Down

Wanna go up,
Never wanna go down.
Wanna take a ride, 'round the whole town.
While flinging flinging flinging everything around.

Wanna go up,
Never wanna go down.
Wanna take a ride, 'round the whole town.
While flinging flinging flinging everything around.

Wanna go up, up, up,
Never wanna go down, down, down.
Wanna take a ride, 'round the whole town, town, town.
While flinging flinging flinging everything around, around,
around.

8. I love to fly

I love to fly on my wings,
I love to fly, fly, fly!
When I fly on my wings,
I feel so happy,
I can fly above the clouds,
I can touch the sky!
Can do all that, 'cause I
Love to fly, fly, fly!
When I touch the sky,
I feel like it's my most blissful moment.
When I fly on my blue transparent wings,
I feel sooo happy!

9. Run Run

Run run run
Motor boat just run run run
Run run run run run run
Just keep runnin'
'Cause we will have to keep
Runnin' all our life life life life life
Run Run
Just keep runnin' so
We will have some fun.
So we will just run along the boat
So that we can have some fun
So So So
Gradually we will build up speed
Just run run we will keep on runnin'

10. Little Doggy

Little Doggy, Little Doggy where do you go?
Oh how I wish I could understand you so.
Little Doggy, Little Doggy let's go play
Oh please tell me what do you say.
I will find out what you say
Even if it costs me the entire day!
Little Doggy, Little Doggy where do you go?
Oh how I wish I could understand you so.

11. Fly Away

This world is fine,
Ain't it divine?
Just walk out the door,
It's time to soar.
Runnin' away,
My umbrella will say;
Just walk out the door,
Umbrella on the floor,
Umbrella's with me,
Yes, I am free!
'Cause all I need,
Is the will, the want,
The brain, the rights
And an umbrella! (long)
'Cause the world's huge
I need to shine in my shoes.
The feelin's great,
I"ll find a way,
To fly, fly, fly away! (x2)

12. Happiness

Everything is happiness,
And joy!
Everything is happiness,
And joy!
I can feel it it it,
Can you you you?
I can feel it it it,
Can you you you?
Happiness and joy,
Are all around me me me,
Maybe around you you you.
Everything is happiness,
And joy!

13. Peace

Peace is needed.
Peace is Peace.
Peace is happiness.
Peace is quietness.
Peace is calmness.
Peace is Peace.

Peace Peace Peace
I need someone with me
Peace Peace Peace
You're Happiness, you're Peace!
Peace Peace Peace
Peace is my favourite,
Peace is somebody else's too.
Peace may not be mine,
Peace may be somebody else's.
But Peace keeps on changing,
Peace Peace Peace.

Peace Peace Peace
I need someone with me
Peace Peace Peace
You're Happiness, you're Peace!
Peace Peace Peace.

14. Fly

So many days have passed by,
How many times have you seen me
Fly fly fly fly?
So many days have passed by,
How many times have you seen me
Fly fly fly fly?
How many times have you seen me
(in a quiet voice) fly like the wind?
How many days have passed by
(high pitch) since you've seen me fly?
How much time had I taken
To fly fly fly fly?
When you see me fly
Along with the clouds,
I feel so happy as I
Touch the clouds!
When I Fly! (long)

15. Lemonade

Do you want to know how to make lemonade?
YES!
Well, let's start!!

Cold ice is nice,
Ice is yummy,
Ice is so very cold;
Ice comes in different shapes too!
Take a glass,
Add a piece or two.
Keep on the side,
Time to move to number 2.

Soooda, fizzy fizzy fizzy soooda,
Soda can be added to your drinks,
To give them an extra pinch,
Don't drink too much of it, though
Take the glass you've filled with ice,
Add a little soda.
Let it fizz,
Come on, let's move on!

Some food you eat,
Is too sweet,
Add some salt,
Eat it up in a jolt!

Salt works like magic!
Take the glass you put ice and soda,
Add half a spoon of salt.
Yummy!

Oh GOD
I forgot
The most important ingredient
That makes the name
It has quite a lot of fame,
Sour sour lemon!
That glass,
Put in half of a lemon,
If you think you want more, put more!

The fluid that makes up
70% of our body,
The tasteless, colourless fluid called water!
Fill the glass full of water,
Voila, your lemonade is ready!
(Don't forget to stir!)

16. The Best Bha in the
World

He is strong,
He is tall,
Tell me who is he, first of all?
He is loving,
He is caring,
With the best smile among all.
He is determined
He is the mastermind
Always supporting me after all.
The lifeline of the house
The shining north star of my life
Who is that? Guesses by all
My dearest brother
My supporter
One in a gazillion… My BHA
Love always,
Little sis.

17. Fruits

Orange on the floor,
That makes me roar.
Apple at the door,
Knockin' in for more.
Banana's being peeled
Now who's it gonna feed?
Grapes come in bunches,
They're not eaten for lunches!
Watermelon being juiced,
Then in a minute it disappeared!
Dragonfruit's sweet,
Different colours to eat!

18. The Watermelon and
the Kiwi

Once there were two companies that were always together.
Their names were the Watermelon and the Kiwi.
They were always together 'cause their founders were best
friends.
(8 seconds pause)
Then suddenly one day they had a very bad rift.
So slowly apart they began to drift.
(8 seconds pause)
Now they are rival companies and I don't know what to do.
For I'm just a narrator narrating their story for you.

19. December 2024

Calendar

January

Sun	Mon	Tue	Wed	Thu	Fri	Sat
26	27	28	29	30	31	1
2	3	4	5	6	7	8
9	10	11	12	13	14	15
16	17	18	19	20	21	22
23	24	25	26	27	28	29
30	31	1	2	3	4	5

February

Sun	Mon	Tue	Wed	Thu	Fri	Sat
30	31	1	2	3	4	5
6	7	8	9	10	11	12
13	14	15	16	17	18	19
20	21	22	23	24	25	26
27	28	1	2	3	4	5
6	7	8	9	10	11	12

March

Sun	Mon	Tue	Wed	Thu	Fri	Sat
27	28	1	2	3	4	5
6	7	8	9	10	11	12
13	14	15	16	17	18	19
20	21	22	23	24	25	26
27	28	29	30	31	1	2
3	4	5	6	7	8	9

April

Sun	Mon	Tue	Wed	Thu	Fri	Sat
27	28	29	30	31	1	2
3	4	5	6	7	8	9
10	11	12	13	14	15	16
17	18	19	20	21	22	23
24	25	26	27	28	29	30
1	2	3	4	5	6	7

May

Sun	Mon	Tue	Wed	Thu	Fri	Sat
1	2	3	4	5	6	7
8	9	10	11	12	13	14
15	16	17	18	19	20	21
22	23	24	25	26	27	28
29	30	31	1	2	3	4
5	6	7	8	9	10	11

June

Sun	Mon	Tue	Wed	Thu	Fri	Sat
29	30	31	1	2	3	4
5	6	7	8	9	10	11
12	13	14	15	16	17	18
19	20	21	22	23	24	25
26	27	28	29	30	1	2
3	4	5	6	7	8	9

July

Sun	Mon	Tue	Wed	Thu	Fri	Sat
26	27	28	29	30	1	2
3	4	5	6	7	8	9
10	11	12	13	14	15	16
17	18	19	20	21	22	23
24	25	26	27	28	29	30
31	1	2	3	4	5	6

August

Sun	Mon	Tue	Wed	Thu	Fri	Sat
31	1	2	3	4	5	6
7	8	9	10	11	12	13
14	15	16	17	18	19	20
21	22	23	24	25	26	27
28	29	30	31	1	2	3
4	5	6	7	8	9	10

September

Sun	Mon	Tue	Wed	Thu	Fri	Sat
28	29	30	31	1	2	3
4	5	6	7	8	9	10
11	12	13	14	15	16	17
18	19	20	21	22	23	24
25	26	27	28	29	30	1
2	3	4	5	6	7	8

October

Sun	Mon	Tue	Wed	Thu	Fri	Sat
25	26	27	28	29	30	1
2	3	4	5	6	7	8
9	10	11	12	13	14	15
16	17	18	19	20	21	22
23	24	25	26	27	28	29
30	31	1	2	3	4	5

November

Sun	Mon	Tue	Wed	Thu	Fri	Sat
30	31	1	2	3	4	5
6	7	8	9	10	11	12
13	14	15	16	17	18	19
20	21	22	23	24	25	26
27	28	29	30	1	2	3
4	5	6	7	8	9	10

December

Sun	Mon	Tue	Wed	Thu	Fri	Sat
27	28	29	30	1	2	3
4	5	6	7	8	9	10
11	12	13	14	15	16	17
18	19	20	21	22	23	24
25	26	27	28	29	30	31
1	2	3	4	5	6	7

December - (long)

December - (long)

December - (long)

Come December, I'll be havin' the time of my life!

December - (long)

December - (long)

December - (long)

Come December, I'll be in Europe by this time!

December - (long)

December - (long)

December - (long)

Come December, I'll be in Disneyland by this time!

December - (long)

December - (long)

December - (long)

Come December, I'll be seeing The Eiffel Tower by this time!

December - (long)

December - (long)

December - (long)

Come December, I'll be skiing by this time!

December - (long)

December - (long)

December - (long)

Come December, I'll be in snow by this time!

20. When the murky waters

(Ta ra ru, rum pa rum,
hu hu)- tune x2
When the murky waters,
Get murkier still.
When the world turns its back,
On you.
When there's nothing but darkness,
ahead.
I'll be the light,
For you.

When the world thinks you're gone,
Away.
When you feel you've been kicked out,
Of it.
I'll be there,
By your side.
After all,
I am your light.
(Tune continues and slowly fades out.)

21. Never judge

Never judge a book by its cover,
Never judge a person by his taste.
Never judge a caterpillar before it transforms,
And never judge a spider by its web.- Chorus

For if you do,
It'll haunt you.
And take your days,
And keep your sleep away.

Life won't be,
That simple for you.
But you'll get through,
Oh don't you worry.

Stop this nonsense,
Stop this madness.
Whether they be mad
Or they be sad,
It's up to them.

(Chorus)

For if you,
Follow these simple rules
You'll find yourself

Appreciating everything.
Life will be,
Much simpler for you.
If you follow,
What this says.
(Chorus in a quiet voice then song over.)

22. A change in me

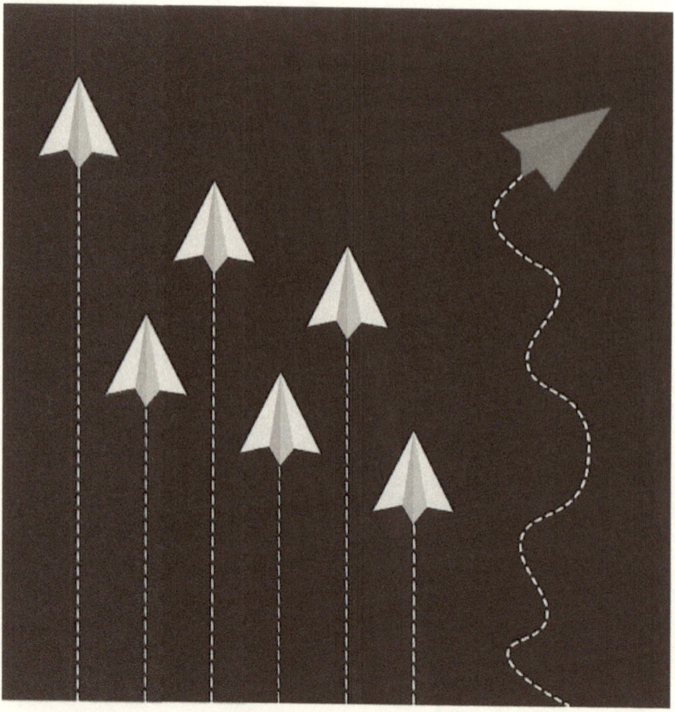

The sun goes down every night.
We all come to play.
We listen to the wind,
That makes our clothes flutter and sway.
Oh yeah oh yeah (x2)
Everyday's just the same,
Except for just one change,
Yeah just one change,
That is a change in me.(long)
Until I achieve all the good qualities,
I'm gonna keep this change with me.
Until the perfect day comes I'll keep it with me.
Yeah with me.(long)

23. Dost - Dosti (a hindi song)

What enmity, yet what friendship!
What enmity, yet what friendship!
The relationship between us is,
What enmity, yet what friendship!

Hum hum, hu hu hum, hu hu hum, hu hu hum.
Hum hum, hu hu hum, hu hu hum, hu hu hum.
Hum hum, hu hu hum, hu hu hum, hu hu hum.

Yaaro, ye dosti hai acchi ya kacchi?
Yaaro, ye dosti hai acchi ya kacchi?
Man ke hai kacche par dosti hai acchi.
Man ke hai kacche par dosti hai acchi.

Hum sab ke din mein ek waqt aata hai.
Hum sab ke din mein ek waqt aata hai.
Padhai - likhai, kitabe aur skool khatam hai.
Padhai - likhai, kitabe aur skool khatam hai.

Hum sab us waqt mein hum kya karte hai?
Hum sab us waqt mein hum kya karte hai?
Mein to mere dosto ke saath khelti hu.
Mein to mere dosto ke saath khelti hu.

Yaaro, ye dosti hai acchi ya kacchi?
Yaaro, ye dosti hai acchi ya kacchi?

Man ke hai kacche par dosti hai acchi.
Man ke hai kacche par dosti hai acchi
Tu ru, tu ru ru, tu ru ruu, tu ru ru.
Tu ru, tu ru ru, tu ru ruu, tu ru ru.
Tu ru, tu ru ru, tu ru ruu, tu ru ru.
(continues and fades out.)

24. Spirit of Diwali

Aaj toh Diwali hai,
Saal ki ek baari hai,
Aaj hum karenge joh
Kise ne nahi kiya, toh,
(beat)
Bolo na kya hoga,
(beat)
Agar dil mein aag joh laga tha,
(beat)
Aaj woh pura kiya
TOH KYAAAAAAA?
Aaj toh Diwali hai,
Saal ki ek baari hai,
Aaj hum karenge joh
Kise ne nahi kiya

25. The Reality of Dreams

Don't get too lost in your dreams cause you'll have to make
'em come true. (fast)
(Yeah ye-yeah!)
Don't get too lost in your dreams, just set the goal and make it
alive. (fast)
(Yeah ye-yeah!)
Don't get too lost in your dreams cause the first thing that
you'll have to do is… (fast)
(WAKE UP!)
Dreams are but a fantasy unless you can make them
otherwise. (fast)
(Yeah ye-yeah!)
Dreams are not the ones you see in sleep. They are the ones
that (keep you awake.) x2 (slow)

26. We Care

We care for environment,
We care, care, care!
We care for plants and trees,
It's always fair!
Cut a tree,
Plant another two,
You can, you can save,
The environment too!

27. Daily Objects

My teddy bear;
Cuddling up at night,
Its so soft
And sweet, and light!
My Kindle;
Its stories never dwindle,
Whether I'm up at night
Or in daylight!
My bottle;
I take it to school,
My grandmother got it
I think it's cool!
My phone charger;
Charges my phone,
When my phone's fully charged
I'm never alone!
My pen stand;
Holds my pen,
Not one, not two
In fact, they're ten!
My pillow;
It holds my head,
In the daytime
Its a cushion instead!